Illustrated History of MARTIAL ARTS

TAE KWON DO

by Jerry Craven

illustrated by Jean Dixon

THE ROURKE CORPORATION, INC.
VERO BEACH, FL 32964

© 1994 The Rourke Corporation, Inc.

Library of Congress Cataloging-in-Publication Data

Craven, Jerry.
    Taekwondo / by Jerry Craven.
       p. cm. — (Illustrated history of martial arts)
    Includes index.
    ISBN 0-86593-367-7
    1. Karate—Juvenile literature. [1. Karate.] I. Title. II. Series.
GV1114.3.C73 1994
796.8'153—dc20
                                   94-4086
                                     CIP
Printed in the USA   AC

TABLE OF CONTENTS

1

THE ORIGINS OF
TAE KWON DO

Tae kwon do is a form of martial arts from Korea. The word means "the way" *(do)* "of kicking" *(tae)* "and punching" *(kwon)*. Not much is known about the early development of the empty-handed fighting that became tae kwon do.

Folk history tells of a prince in India about 5,000 years ago who developed a way of fighting. He found the vulnerable spots in the human body in a grisly way. He stabbed slaves in various parts of their bodies to discover the best spots for killing or crippling. Then he designed punches and kicks that targeted these spots.

About 1,400 years ago, an Indian Buddhist monk named Bodhidharma moved to China, where he introduced Zen Buddhism to the Chinese. He taught his traveling monks self-defense exercises to strengthen them for hard journeys and to protect them from bandits.

People of all ages enjoy tae kwon do as a sport. The youngest in this photograph is four years old. At age 73, Petie Clapper, a woman living in Florida, earned a black belt in tae kwon do.

Ancient Korean warriors wore armor made from wood, so many fighters learned to break wood with a kick. Board breaking is still a part of tae kwon do today.

Some historians date the spread of martial arts in Asia from the followers of Bodhidharma. The fighting form they practiced for self-defense was called *kwon bop*. Perhaps monks took kwon bop to Korea, Japan and Okinawa.

Many Koreans believe that the martial art ancestor of tae kwon do was Korean, not Indian or Chinese. Koreans point out that there are statues of men in tae kwon do stances carved in rock that date hundreds of years before the coming of Bodhidharma and the Zen monks. It is possible that tae kwon do developed almost entirely in Korea.

2

THE HWARANG WARRIORS AND

T A E K   K W O N

A group of warriors called the Hwarang was important in the early development of tae kwon do. This group originated in Silla, the smallest of the three kingdoms in the Korean peninsula before unification at the end of the seventh century.

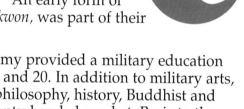

At first the Hwarang were trained in an academy for the sons of the nobility. They studied *Hwarang-do,* which means "the way of blossoming manhood." An early form of tae kwon do, called *taek kwon,* was part of their training.

The Hwarang academy provided a military education for men between ages 16 and 20. In addition to military arts, the young men studied philosophy, history, Buddhist and Confucian ethics, and empty-handed combat. Basic to the teaching of the academy were five rules of conduct. These came from the teaching of a Buddhist scholar. These rules were:

- loyalty to country
- obedience to parents
- loyalty to comrades
- steadfastness in battle
- justice in taking life in battle

Part of the competition in modern tae kwon do is form. These two boys perform tae kwon do exercises before a judge at an official tournament.

From its ancient origins as a form of serious combat, tae kwon do has developed into a sport. Participants wear protective gear to avoid injury.

The five rules of conduct provided a structure for moral living for the Hwarang. Thus their training in martial arts helped prepare them for life, not just for war.

The Hwarang also learned to recite poetry, to sing and to dance. Such skills were deemed important if young men were to have civilized social grace. A part of their education was travel to see how different people lived.

The traveling warriors of Silla helped spread the knowledge of their martial art, taek kwon, throughout the Korean peninsula.

3

EARLY DEVELOPMENT OF

T A E K W O N D O

Some historians say that 1,400 years ago, the elite warriors of the Hwarang academy in Silla learned a fighting style called *soo bak.* Then, to improve their skills, they studied how wild animals fought. They adapted offensive and defensive tactics of the animals to improve their own hand-to-hand combat.

The warriors added what they learned from animals to earlier empty-handed combat to form the style called taek kwon. Others claim that taek kwon was introduced to the Hwarang by the military force of another kingdom, sent to help fight pirates.

Warriors also added to their fighting skills the techniques of meditation used by the Zen Buddhists. Meditation helped the warriors focus and concentrate.

The result of the combination of soo bak, animal fighting styles, and Zen meditation was a highly effective early form of tae kwon do called *soo bak do,* or "the way of punching and butting." Supposedly it was this fighting style that helped the warrior class who developed it to defeat all enemies and unite the entire Korean peninsula for the first time.

The Koryo dynasty maintained peace in Korea (which was named after the Koryo family). Warriors refined soo bak do until it was more than a fighting art. During over 400 years without civil war, the warriors used soo bak do as both a way to stay healthy and as a competitive sport.

By the late 1300s, soo bak do became a popular sport among the public. King Chongjo published a book on martial arts. He considered soo bak do as the most important style.

While ancient warriors sought to kill or injure one another, modern combatants using tae kwon do have a referee to enforce rules and prevent injury. Here the referee is calling a foul for a kick to the knee.

DECLINE AND

R
E
B
I
R
T
H

Taek kwon, developed in the military academy for training Hwarang warriors, became known as soo bak. People in peacetime turned to soo bak for recreation and exercise.

Korean martial art became less and less an art for warriors, especially during the Yi dynasty (1397-1907). Throughout the country, people turned to other activities and neglected the study of martial arts. By the early 20th century, few knew anything about taek kwon or soo bak. A few families practiced soo bak, but they kept the knowledge secret.

The Koreans experienced a rebirth in interest in martial arts when Japan invaded their country in 1909. One of the first acts of the ruling Japanese army general was to ban the study and practice of martial arts.

Korean patriots traveled to isolated Buddhist temples to learn soo bak. Some young men went to China and others went to Japan to study martial arts.

By the time Korea was liberated from Japanese rule at the end of World War II, many Koreans had learned different martial arts. Traditional taek kwon, or soo bak, was influenced by *judo, karate, kung fu* and other forms of combat.

The first school to teach Korean martial arts in the 20th century opened in 1945 in Seoul. This school was named the Chung Do Kwan. Soon other major schools opened, each claiming to teach the official traditional martial art native to Korea.

SEOUL

Today, the World Tae Kwon Do Federation has its headquarters in the city of Seoul in South Korea.

While most people practice tae kwon do as a competitive sport, it is also an effective form of self-defense.

5

INFLUENCE OF THE KOREAN

C O N F L I C T

By the time the United States became involved in the Korean Conflict, a dozen schools in Seoul, South Korea, claimed to teach traditional martial arts. However, the masters at the schools disagreed on what styles of fighting made up the correct native Korean martial art.

In 1952, two events took place that helped unify the different schools.

One event was a demonstration of martial arts performed for the president of South Korea, Syngman Rhee. The president was so impressed that he told the military to make taek kwon a part of every soldier's training.

The other event was a demonstration in the United States. A martial arts master arrived in Fort Benning, Georgia, to study radio electronics. While in school, the master gave a public demonstration of taek kwon. This was the beginning of American interest in Korean martial arts.

During the Korean Conflict, a special South Korean commando group called the Black Tigers learned taek kwon. They often penetrated into North Korea, sometimes as assassins.

Noah Goodson teaches tae kwon do in Texas. He says his training is typical of many tae kwon do teachers who learned martial arts while in the United States Army. Master Goodson holds black belts in karate and tae kwon do.

Tae kwon do training includes ways to block an attack. This is one form of the X block. It is good for protecting against attacks to the face.

After the war, the 29th infantry division of the South Korean army established Che Ju Island as its headquarters. There, all Korean soldiers received training in taek kwon.

6

THE NAME

OF THE ART

In the 20th century, masters of martial arts in Korea struggled with identity. They wanted to teach the true and original Korean martial art. By the middle of the century, it was apparent to many that the ancient fighting art developed in Korea had been influenced by the martial arts of many countries, especially China and Japan. The influences included judo, kung fu, karate and others.

Nevertheless, Korean masters wanted a Korean name for their art. They also wanted to teach something distinctive, something different from the martial arts of other countries. So in 1955, masters from schools all over South Korea met to discuss the identity for the martial art of Korea.

They decided on the name *tae soo do*. Most of the masters also decided to work at making techniques of kicking, punching and blocking the basis of their art.

Two years after selecting the name tae soo do, the masters met again and changed the name to tae kwon do. Most felt that the new name better described their art. Also, it sounded more like "taek kwon," which had been used for centuries.

The main event for a tae kwon do meet is sparring. For determining who wins, judges value kicks more than punches.

14

This tae kwon do master is yelling as a part of a sparring match. The yell serves two purposes: (1) to help the one yelling focus on technique, and (2) to unnerve the opponent.

Even with a common name and some dedication to teaching similar techniques, many masters disagreed on standards. It soon became apparent to all that they needed a governing board to help with rules and to spread the teaching of tae kwon do.

7 ORGANIZING

When the masters of the various schools (called *kwans)* first met in 1955 to decide on a name, not everyone agreed. Some even disagreed about the basic movements of the art. However, only one other form of martial art in Korea is generally recognized as a legitimate native form. It is called *hapkido.* However, it did not gain the national and international attention given to tae kwon do.

A number of masters of kwans got together in 1961 to form the Korean Tae Kwon Do Association. They had several goals. One was to set standards for competition. Another was to help spread the teaching of Korea's special brand of martial art.

The Korean Tae Kwon Do Association sent teachers to many countries. The teachers put on demonstrations, attracting much attention to their art. People liked the drama of punches and the high kicks. Students, especially in high schools and colleges, began asking for instruction in tae kwon do.

During the Vietnam War, South Vietnamese government officials asked the Korean Tae Kwon Do Association to send masters to teach soldiers. By 1970, many people throughout the world knew of tae kwon do.

Under the leadership of the official Korean organization, masters set up gymnasiums for teaching tae kwon do in dozens of countries. These gymnasiums were called *dojangs,* and they were open to the public.

TAE KWON DO

Here a contestant scores with a kick. In tae kwon do sparring, contestants must wear headgear, chest protection, and padding for forearms and shins.

THE WORLD
FEDERATION

With the aid of the Korean Tae Kwon Do Association, a new organization formed in 1973. This was the World Tae Kwon Do Federation.

It was the goal of the new organization to spread the teaching of tae kwon do and to maintain standards. The federation was also necessary to help set up matches around the world.

In 1973 Seoul, with the aid of the world federation, hosted the first world championship tae kwon do matches. Many countries have since hosted the world championship matches, including Germany, Denmark, South Africa and the United States.

The South Korean government has given official recognition to the World Tae Kwon Do Federation. With support from both the international organization and the government, tae kwon do achieved recognition by the International Olympic Committee.

In 1988, when the Olympic Games were held in South Korea, the Olympic Committee designated tae kwon do as an official demonstration sport. When the world watched the 1988 Olympics, people all over the globe became fascinated with the high kicks of tae kwon do.

Along with karate, tae kwon do is the most popular martial art in the world. Children as young as four enjoy the sport. People well into their 60s find tae kwon do keeps them limber and young.

More than 20 million people now practice tae kwon do. These people live in over 140 different countries. The popularity of tae kwon do continues to grow.

Here a contestant breaks a board with a kick. Board breaking was a skill valued by fighters centuries ago when Korean soldiers wore armor made of wood.

9

COMPETITIVE

Tae kwon do competitors match their skills against others in their belt classes. These, listed in order of skill, are white, yellow, green, blue, red and black.

The most dramatic contest in a competitive meet is the sparring. For each match, there are one or two jurors, two judges, a timekeeper and a referee.

Competitors wear protective headgear and a padded vest. The body area that is covered by the vest is the only area fist strikes are allowed. Open-handed blows are prohibited. Foot blows may hit both body and head, but not the neck.

Judges award one point for any fist or foot strike that lands solidly in legal areas. Usually, the winner is the one who scores the most points (see box).

In the case of a tie in points, judges award the match to the competitor deemed superior. Some of the guidelines judges use in tied scores are:

1. foot strikes are superior to fist strikes;
2. a jumping kick is superior to a standing kick;
3. a counterattack is superior to an initiated attack.

There are other areas of competition besides sparring. In competitive meets, contestants can win trophies for form and for demonstrating skill at breaking boards with high kicks.

In the board-breaking competition, a competitor kicks a one-inch pine board held at head height. Kicking a board with enough power to break it demonstrates mastery of body control and coordination.

TAE KWON DO

This girl is scoring a point with a kick.

YOU WIN A TAE KWON DO MATCH IF:

1. You score more points.
2. Your opponent withdraws.
3. The referee disqualifies your opponent.
4. You knock your opponent out in a legal attack.
5. Your opponent is injured in a legal attack.
6. The referee stops the contest to award you the match.

10

THE

K
N
I
F
E

F
O
O
T

Though both feet and hands are important, tae kwon do emphasizes kicks over strikes with the hand or fist.

The tae kwon do fighter uses five areas of the foot for striking an opponent. Many high kicks use the part of the foot called "the knife." This is the area on the outside edge of the foot, used especially for side kicks and kicks to the instep, knee, abdomen, head and neck.

Tae kwon do teaches striking with other parts of the foot. One is the ball of the foot, used in round and front kicks to the knee, groin, stomach, abdomen, chest, neck, face and temple.

The back, the side and the bottom of the heel are also used for striking. The bottom of the heel is good for stamping, while the other parts of the heel are effective for kicks delivered when spinning on the other foot.

The arch of the foot is used in striking the arms and face. It is also used to block attacks.

The instep is an effective weapon for attacking the groin, face, temple and neck.

In sparring, it is not permissible to kick places where the opponent might be seriously injured, such as the neck. However, tae kwon do masters teach the more dangerous techniques for use in self-defense.

Judges prepare to award trophies at the end of a tae kwon do meet.

In tae kwon do, the outside edge of the foot is called the "knife foot."

11

PROPER

STANCE

**HORSES,
CATS
AND
CRANES**

Stance is important in tae kwon do. In order to be able to punch and kick, a person must have proper balance. The person who launches an attack from the wrong stance risks losing balance – and falling or being knocked down.

There are 15 fundamental stances in tae kwon do, as well as a number of others used by advanced students. Among the basic stances are two variations of the horseback stance. These provide proper balance for both kicks and straight fist punches. A person standing in the horseback stance looks like he is riding a horse.

The contestant on his knees is recovering from a painful kick while his opponent stands, back turned, in an at-ease position, waiting for the timekeeper to end the timeout.

The horseback stance provides stability and balance. It is good for defending against an attack as well as for launching an attack.

The cat stance is a dramatic crouch. It prepares a person to move fast, either to attack or to defend against a rear attack by spinning around.

The crane stance resembles the position assumed by the hero in the movie *The Karate Kid,* as he launched into his high kick to win the karate tournament at the end of the movie. The crane stance is also useful in defense, especially in blocking both high and low attacks from the side.

Among the advanced stances are the mountain and mountain cliff. Both are useful in blocking. Mountain is for high side blocks, and mountain cliff allows the use of both high and low blocks.

THE

K
N
I
F
E

H
A
N
D

As a weapon in tae kwon do, the hand has many unusual names, depending on how it is used. It can be "a spear," "a knife" or "a hammer." Other hand positions have even stranger names, such as "chicken beak," "bear" and "pincer."

In tae kwon do, the clenched fist is the most often-used striking weapon. There are, in fact, eight different ways to close the fingers to make a fist. The most common is the forefist, made by closing the fingers and bringing the thumb against the index and middle fingers. Most blows with the forefist start beside the hip as a thrust with the palm up.

There are 10 different finger positions for open-handed blows.

When most people think of a "karate chop," they envision the knife hand. In tae kwon do, the knife hand is effective for both attacking and blocking. The striking area on the knife hand is the muscle between the base of the little finger and the wrist. Knife hand strikes are made both with palm up and palm down. Such blows are most effective against the ribs, abdomen, collarbone, temple, neck and face.

In tournaments, only closed fist blows are allowed. Fist strikes must be directed only against protected areas of the body below the neck.

Both girls and boys enjoy the competition of a tae kwon do tournament.

The knife hand block is useful against attacks to the middle section of the body.

13
MEDITATION

A person who wants to be good at tae kwon do must learn to concentrate. When facing an attack it is important to be aware – but not to think about yourself in ways that distract you.

Tae kwon do meditation helps people learn to concentrate. The techniques sound easy, but for those who have never tried meditating, it can be difficult. It is best to practice meditation while you are still, and then learn to do it while moving.

To meditate while still, relax mentally. Don't try to figure anything out, and don't allow yourself to be curious about anything. If you wish, close your eyes. Try not to think about anything in particular.

This four-year-old boy is practicing sparring with his father before facing an opponent in a tae kwon do tournament.

Most people prefer to practice meditation while sitting.

If you choose to sit, cross your legs, and keep your knees close to the floor. Do not force the position or you will become distracted by discomfort. Keep your back straight and rest your hands on your knees.

If you kneel to meditate, put your knees together and relax against your feet. Place your palms on your thighs; keep your back straight.

If you stand, do so with your feet shoulder-width apart and cross your hands over your belt.

If meditation is difficult, try thinking about your breathing. Imagine seeing the air come into you as a silver thread.

If you practice proper meditation, you can do a better job with the complicated moves of tae kwon do.

14

TAE KWON DO

TODAY

Tae kwon do has become one of the most popular martial arts around the world. Some argue that it is a sport rather than a true martial art. Certainly tae kwon do is effective in self-defense. Maybe it is the sports aspects of tae kwon do that make it more popular than other martial arts. People tend to like competitive meets where trophies are awarded for skills.

The World Tae Kwon Do Federation has promoted the popularity of tae kwon do by sending demonstration teams all over the world. It also sets rules for meets and offers official sanction for tournaments that meet its standards.

Such rules help keep the teaching of tae kwon do uniform, while the popularity of the sport means there are plenty of schools. Even in most small communities in the United States, there are teachers who give private tae kwon do lessons.

Competitive sparring is the most popular part of every tae kwon do tournament.

Hwarang-do: literally meaning "the way of blossoming manhood," this was a seventh-century form of martial art that later developed into tae kwon do.

kwans: schools or places of learning.

kwon bop: a form of self-defense used by Buddhist monks 1,400 years ago.

martial arts: any form of military training; often the term refers to empty-handed fighting, as well as to the various forms of exercises and sports developed from ancient fighting skills.

soo bak: a form of fighting practiced by Silla 1,400 years ago.

taek kwon: an early form of tae kwon do.

tae soo do: the name Korean masters in the 20th century agreed upon for the traditional form of empty-handed fighting; they changed the name to tae kwon do.

X block: a tae kwon do defensive move performed by crossing the arms at the wrist.

GLOSSARY

INDEX